THE

CITY

SHE

WAS

The Mountain West Poetry Series
Stephanie G'Schwind & Donald Revell, series editors

We Are Starved, by Joshua Kryah
The City She Was, by Carmen Giménez Smith

THE

CITY

SHE

WAS

POEMS

Carmen Giménez Smith

The Center for Literary Publishing
Colorado State University

For information about permission to reproduce
selections from this book, write to
Permissions, Center for Literary Publishing,
9105 Campus Delivery, Department of English,
Colorado State University,
Fort Collins, Colorado 80523-9105.

Printed in the United States of America.

Library of Congress Cataloging-in-Publication Data

Giménez Smith, Carmen, 1971-
The city she was : poems / Carmen Giménez Smith.
p. cm. -- (The Mountain West poetry series)
Includes bibliographical references.
ISBN 978-1-885635-19-8 (pbk. : alk. paper)
ISBN 978-1-885635-23-5 (electronic)
I. Title.

PS3607.I45215C58 2011
811'.6--dc22

2011037729

The paper used in this book meets the minimum requirements of the American
National Standard for Information Sciences-Permanence of Paper for Printed Library
Materials, ANSI Z39.48-1984.

1 2 3 4 5   15 14 13 12 11

Publication of this book was made possible by a grant from
the National Endowment for the Arts.

ART WORKS.
arts.gov

To Jack Bunting and Larisa Chapman

CONTENTS

One

Two

Three

ONE

For About Five Minutes in the Aughts

I put up notice on the Internet where misspellers wrote the most compelling notes.
They wore industrial eyeglasses and ironic T-shirts and trucker hats
and often forgot their wallets. One taught me about science fiction porn
while we lay on his silk leopard-print sheets. After that, a Nugent
look-alike, then a mapmaker in Alaska and that old-timey
going-nowhere correspondence; I thought I'd tell our kids about our cute meet
over Thanksgiving in the new fifties. I watched films that made me feel old
because of choice feminism contradictions and wrote poems about
the city's howling lunatics in technology and snark dialect compost.
And then, and then, and then. Met a lunatic on Craigslist.
Concerned about starts, I stuffed his inbox with amendments and bloated metonymy.
This happened for months. This happened while I healed from pneumonia,
from broken bones, from agoraphobia. Drinking beer gave me a panic, so whiskey.
Divorce ephemera, safe doors and pre-midlife. I collected fancy pens
and *yeah, I'm working on an article about animé and Marxism.* Pills
made me shaky, but I filled myself with pills because they made me shaky.
Attended dotcom parties thrown by post-Stanford nerds in tucked-in shirts,
such Adam's apples. They gave away fonty tchotchkes for Internet pet stores
and other terrible ideas. Just one hayride after the next and only tickling
and stalker calling, the hang-up thing. We'd work on it,
we'd patch it up. My action item, my best of bread.
I met the lunatic and we did it until it outlived its hipness,
until it was Eastern European. We did it until the buildings came down.
We did it until the affect was moot, until the recipe got muddled.
We did it until I turned into myself, until the whole city turned into itself.
We did it until the line got too long and therapy turned me down. I'm talking
Beginning of the Decline of Our Smug Empire. I'm talking
about the rise of a collective posture for the skittering tower of our time.

Pills

This one softens the soul cartilage.
This one makes the red lights green.
I have bought enough powder
to make a tiny little cartoon cat.
Mitsubishi, Batman, Teletubby, Toyota:
I love you. I love the Earth and forgive it.
I love you: guy at the weird apartment
playing South Park video games, guy
with tennis scholarship and the guy
who has a grandmother who's dying
because you all carry. You make me
love helicopters and dust.

This one makes me throw up, but then
I listen to Pink Floyd in the dark without
getting scared. This one throws a dart
at my nemesis, but it's a lame gesture.
This one makes my augmentation less brutal.
The doctor gives me one that says,
this might cause sudden death. 250 mg vs 500 mg.
Dry mouth, nausea, dizziness.
This one is legal, so it's not as fun.
Take this one with orange juice.
Swallow this one with a spoonful of peanut butter.
Take this one alone. Don't take this one alone.
This one brings the horizon line into your lexicon,
and you store it for better occasions.

Chewing this puts me on a raft on Lake Erie.
I'm in the sun, then I'm in the mud baths
of Black Rock City getting felt up by a chick
with a bone in her nose, then I'm at the top
of the hill of my street getting the mail,

no business driving, then I'm alone
under the single bulb of self-interrogation.
This one makes me near-dead but still pretty.
This one makes my friends hate me.
This one makes my friends hating me
a dull sting, calamine lotion for the brain.
If I take this one, then I can bury
the undead with a spoon. This one
belongs in a hall of fame. The last one
not really the last one,
the one I want to relish, my first Casanova.

The Walk

Like a wino I trolled the streets
in search of an elixir for my
melancholy. A Virgo with gold
teeth lured me into his lap
and sang songs about the fraudulent
landscape. *The purple sky*
is invented for you. The purple
sky is not among us. When his hand
traveled south, I blushed.
I left when tomorrow made sense.
That's the way a walk renews—
she makes her way through
the imperfect city and discovers
how the world is people
with hand puppets. People who shiver
metal sheets for thunder,
and then she squints her eyes
to fuzz it more, to prettify.

Vita

- The ladies at the laundromat called me La Chula for my role on the show *Trainwreck*. I had birds in my hair and my porcelain feet chipped when walking. An earthquake and, an omen, the Emmy for *Best Hooker with a Heart of Gold Ingénue* fell on me as I slept.

- Later I sold chocolate smuggled in from Morocco, but it was so boring I faked my own death. Muffling my voice with a hanky, I called in as weeping mother. For days, I cried thinking about the things I hadn't gotten to do like jump from planes or have sex with British DJs.

- My lover said *massage school*. He said *PhD*.

- Then I built Taj Mahal replicas with dried pasta and sold them to Texas Junior Leaguers for thousands of dollars. I was moody and dark and skinny and *Modern Painters* did a feature on me. I posed on the roof of my building with a mannequin. I poured hot water on one of my works, and the photographer and I ate it.

- After this, I professionally wrestled men and my ring name was Kristeva the Krusher because I was brutal and post-feminist. The league paid me in Macy's gift cards, so I could buy lacy garments and complicate the paradigm.

- *Without training, you won't go places,* my lover said. *Without an education you'll work where they can't remember your name,* he said. *It's not you. It's the edifice and me, our default. We're keeping you out on purpose because we only really like you in bits.*

- That year, I learned Pet through the mail from Sally Struthers who also spoke King Cobra, and I counseled cats although I was allergic. The cats argued that their reputation for indifference left them love-starved, but I talked over them because this was true for me, too.

- I squandered a date with Ms. R.G. Destiny by being too breathy and insistent. With Mr. Great Hair, I was sprightly and I lay open like the library dictionary. I used words like *journey* and *spirit* in earnest like I had crystals and an altar to Gaia. Like that.

- At that time I invested too much in the thing itself. I should have diversified. I fell into every role offered to me.

- My résumé was a phone book, a travel guide or a Bible, a vacuum cleaner with no money down. I sold those, too. If retrospect were a lifestyle, then I would be jet set. If regret were a whistle, then I'd be its dog. I'd be the dog trainer mauled by the dog, plotting my workmen's compensation package while selling underwear at middle-class ladies' parties.

Museum of Lost Acquaintance

We'll be erasing the past, so I'll insist on paying. You'll stare at me with brace face and forgive me.

Whisper that secret name we learned from the movies. I'll forgive you.

We'll puppet voices and mug shots, and you can forgive and forget. We'll bury our past.

We'll surprise your grandmother's house with paint. Grateful, you'll return
the sweater you said you lost at the Mormon dance.

I'll live under a blanket.

We'll wear matching Izods to Sadie's Dance and french by the trophy case.

I'll show you pictures of my dog. We can walk through the mall and pierce our ears.

We'll deliver pizzas in a white Corolla. We'll take the bus or catch a ride with a
stranger who strokes my bra strap. You'll ride my handlebars or I on the back of
your Vespa.

We'll try for summer jobs with the city and not find any. We'll listen to the Doors
and pretend it's the sixties. We'll pretend we do drugs and surf. Your dad will drive
us to the boardwalk to buy skateboards.

You'll reject my boyfriends and I'll reject your girlfriends.

We'll pretend to like each other's lovers.

We'll pretend to understand poetry and carry notebooks on buses and talk in fake
accents.

We'll decide to start a Bauhaus tribute band but quit because we fight over who'll be
lead singer. You'll start one behind my back, I behind yours.

I'll drive you to your abortion, you to mine.

Sometimes we'll build houses for poor people and be noble.

And then we'll be yuppies and have titles at our jobs with nine words in them like Asia Pacific Manager of Development for Future Projects Millennium.

We'll have another wedding.

We'll quit our jobs and go to grad school. I'll major in Women's Studies, you in Labor Law.

We'll live off the grid. We'll live sort of off the grid and spend too much money on organic marmalade.

I'll fuck your boyfriend, and you'll fuck my brother.

I'll stake out your house, read your journal, smell your hair while you sleep.

You'll throw all my clothes in Glad Bags and we'll have a big dramatic fight like in that perfume commercial. We'll make sex tapes.

We'll meet guys online and send them pictures of your sister.

We'll buy out-of-date garments and decorate them with spangles and feathers because we want to be pretty.

We'll say nice things we don't mean, bust in on frenemies, chap our lips from snow. Cave into peer pressure.

We'll put you in your first suit with a tie from the eighties.

Do you know how to give yourself a tattoo? You can give me one, too.

I will drive you to the mountains and off a cliff into and against the trees.

Some of it will be true and some of it will test what we know.

Some of the things we do together will disturb our fragile social circle. We'll escape the fragile social circle for your garage.

Some of the time, I will like the nights when we don't talk for hours until we're facing in bed.

Some of it will feel awkward like before we knew what each other's ears looked like close up.

We'll go to pretend jail to lift weights and make shanks from toothbrushes.

At times we'll hate so much that it becomes its own living thing.

At times I will drive addled for you. At times you'll walk up a thousand stairs.

Turn me in, offer me coffee, take me soup, and privilege my opinion.

You'll teach me soccer like you said you would. I'll take you to Los Angeles to look for Perry Farrell and you'll claim you saw him and I'll pretend to believe you because that's what it was all about in the first place, the believing.

I'll greet you in the Chinese restaurant where I was pretty and you weren't.

You'll greet me in the pool hall where I was fat and you weren't.

It'll be conciliatory. We'll feel like we can't talk. We'll take a bath together.

We'll move in and away from each other. It'll be like we never happened before.

The City She Was

1.
Longing brings me to the bar.
Smoke swirling draws me in.
This could get serial.

We use wine goblets as mirrors
when we talk about war.
We're trying at sophistication.

My head is the sound
of a body's erosion.
Five minutes from defilement,
and I snap like it's a fancy.
They don't know
me from my body on them.

After a speck of morning light,
my amnesia thickens,
then rises like bile.

2.
The city depends
on being the most *something*.
The string of shoes
from the phone wires:
cryptic odes to hometowns.
It's morning so we crowd the bus stations
to earn our pittance, the dream life.

3.
The city's eye
revises my face,
so that fluorescence

makes an illegal, a yuppie,
a salesgirl or an angel
of the hole I make in the fog.

4.
Throw romance
over a bridge, through a toll,
in the alley, under the billboard,
to the curled fingers on the window,
kicked to the curb, off-ramp past
the homeless
with the wilted sign.
Pamphlet the whole city
with your tractate.

5.
The day is bare as white,
so I stay inside
lest the wind change me.
I sort my miniskirts to trade
with skinny girls at Buffalo Exchange.
The shops along the avenue
offer new strategies:
to be modern or demure.
Minx or Library.
I could be the whole beachside,
cold and bleak and briny
but homey nonetheless.

6.
Loneliness hides
in a corner to tell me
about the troubles he had

finding a place to park his self.
He's my new fellow
and brings me flowers wrapped
in indie weeklies denouncing
how we live
purchasing and fading.

7.
One street into,
and three away—
we're treading fiscal boundaries:
one building with blue trim
and one with tin shingles.
The houses project
their occupants.
Where there is decay, failure,
catastrophic or slowly
wearing, and where there is
gleam, atonement.
Desire turned into itself,
made saccharine.

8.
Civic melancholy
pushes through the traffic, so
I don't see right
in this Babel.
If I owned the city,
so little of it would be.
I pass over the avenue,
assemble some ending of mine
as a vision or a refusal.

Bleeding Heart

My heart is bleeding. It bleeds upward and fills
my mouth up with salt. It bleeds because of a city in ruins,
the chair still warm from sister's body,
because it will all be irreproducible. My heart
is bleeding because of baby bear not finding mama bear and it bleeds
to the tips of my fingers like I painted my nails Crimson.
Sometimes my heart bleeds so much I am a raisin.
It bleeds until I am a quivering ragged clot, bleeds at the ending
with the heroine and her sunken cancer eyes, at the ending
with the plaintive flute over smoke-choked killing fields. I'm bleeding
a river of blood right now and it's wearing a culvert in me for the blood. My heart
rises up in me, becomes the cork of me and I choke on it. I am bleeding
for you and for me and for the tiny babies and the IED-blown
leg. It bleeds because I'm made that way, all filled up with blood,
my sloppy heart a sponge filled with blood to squeeze onto
any circumstance. Because it is mine, it will always bleed.
My heart bled today. It bled onto the streets
and the steps of city hall. It bled in the pizza parlor with the useless jukebox.
I've got so much blood to give inside and outside of any milieu.
Even for a bad zoning decision, I'll bleed so much you'll be bleeding,
all of us bleeding in and out like it's breathing,
or kissing, and because it is righteous and terrible and red.

Division

The fantasy: to lure you into a bush to tear out your heart.

These heart trades: my poor impulse control for your eroding face. The prize: territory.

Living provincial is hard; navigating restaurants with sharks in them is harder.

I want horrorcore-pique. I want to break your bones with mind or contempt.

Which would be more effective? We're so talented at protracted and foaming slowkill.

Our thing was like a box of chocolates with razors in them.

Our thing was like a factory of soul-slicing. We put souls on hooks. We pushed them through grinders.

We deforest, we slay with biting humor, and wait for what is offered in return.

It's what we vow because we're caught in each other's complex web.

TWO

The Science of Parting

You're a wet thing in my throat: oyster.
Particulate matter too: oyster and earth.
If I mix it, then you're planet, the meniscus
so bright to burn me. You're a ruddy neck,
porous and freckle. You're opalescent
material in the fathoms, the genus of which
I am branch. You're the knitting of scars, that miracle.
I sit in the kitchen, and you're the compound of rain and wind
on our windows. I pin myself to your axis, sure and solid
gradient. You're the Cartesian pause in my basis,
the cog sound of mechanical doors aching
with exit. Then later, you're my recurrence,
the integer that began us, the formula, its solution.

Beauty Regimen

The bottles and tubes on my vanity
make my room a factory with no union.
I'm the scab, eager for a few nickels.
I build piecework in and around hangers.
I'll find the face in the marble if I'm diligent,
reads the affirmation in the mirror.

I rinse my face's one thousand minutes
and look for the mistakes, which is not to say
I'm not beautiful. If I could finish with erasure,
I'd prop my face on a stand to keep the dust from it.

Before bed I look at women's magazines
for myself, an old familiar slice. I rub envelope
fragrances against my neck like they're mash notes
about the slippery inference of my lips.

The TV casts its viridian glare, makes me
a tepid silhouette against the mouse hole.
The hole's a shadow tunnel into my chest,
one-way ticket. If only diligence were love.

The Grand Tour

The king is slain, small death since
we used his porn as atlas. Each scene
was our next frontier and we crossed it.
Now he is all tumescent cat eyes, petulance.

He says, *My mother never
smiled, I'm always lonely.* It's *blah blah
blah.* It's *therefore, therefore.*
The headboard's made of driftwood
and Xmas lights, and I just want to kiss
and smoke clove cigarettes like we used to.
Give me the hasty shower and the smell of Dr. Bronner's.

I want to be the thinking I invented last night,
but I've already run out of disguise.
Instead it's some amour, plush velvet,
some pretending to read Proust. We're propping
up the corpse of romantic love.

This king is really here to cut his teeth
on our asymmetry. *Everyone smiles,*
I answer because we've already split
the floorboards with our ruckus.
We're in the shipwreck on the deserted island
and the king's a parrot cawing *shore, shore.*

We're containers told in clay with nice faces
when they orphan our hours for maps:
exteriors to decorate with unction and indigo.

We get sexy over island domination.
The island is inside us: the birth of empire,
its crooks and its courts.
Islands, always the story.

Pageant of Scrutiny

The women at the laundromat across the street fret over their modes of transport (shopping cart, duffel, canvas tote, plastic bin). Because I'm their spectator, framed in my window, I'm also a talisman against cages. They sit outside of their labors to watch me watch them. I'm their poppet, so they interrogate my hermitage. *It's because of love,* says the kind one and the cruel one says, *it's because of impertinence,* and the conciliatory one says, *it's all those things, but perhaps we shouldn't judge since she's just like us, etc.,* and the compassionate one says, *let's send her up a ladder,* and the drunk one says, *I wonder who the hell she comes around,* and the one with a wimple trimmed in blue said, *I wish it was me,* and along comes the other one, the angry one: *if we'd have quit smoking in the sixties, not given ourselves over, I've got an idea, let's start a posse, unfurl the cue cards,* so that it seems she's taken over, and she has—the other ones tend to her, purge me from their crosshairs. I'm the one who used to look in windows and say, *she just does it to herself because she's a sucker and the void has such a sexy pitch in his voice.* I used to wash my clothes in that place, took it wrapped in a sheet like a corpse of want and discharge and worry. To alleviate ourselves of filth we moved around the small hall of machines, banged at the change machine when the monotony rage came on. In the laundromat we were strangers but also repentant and transgressive. From my perch the women seem like specks now. *We go, we go.* They're all complicit with my cage. I'd trade all my seeds for a gust out of these millennial doldrums. The tossing swish of the machine might be the best trade in town.

The Skeptic

endless is so big a country—
still there's something soft
in God's line of reason
that pulls on
the part that longs
for an end
right out of me

maybe it's that
this gets repeated
in perpetuity
presenting me to
the idea we are
both far away
and right upon it

In-Between Elegy

We had—one chance lined up on the museum bench—examining a Kay Sage
painting of doors and robes—

it's quiet enough for contemplating an undoing—we stood knee deep in a bog
of our own making—

heretofore handled one another like grandmother's horse figurine—even cleaned
with our own raggeds—needing the fortress we were—

and then to chip away at—to bear down onto—to find the holes and tear them
larger—that would be the collaboration—

If there had only been pauses—if only we had desisted in the tumble
downward—I mean we clipped sisyphus and jill—made eddies we could not see
to see—

we were analysis and question—secrets forested—both imbued in poems—
lies we thought at the time were—

And I might have thought—commenting on the museum-goers instead—
the one with the turquoise belt—the one with the diaphanous hair a halo round
her—

that this is—what terrible endings were—your hand over me—dining with its
spoon fingers—the meat on my neck's bones—

The Endangered You

Because the you slipped from me like a bead of mercury. Sometimes it was a big you with long gray hair and other times it was a young man with a curl on his forehead, a vicious girl in a bathtub.

The you had burrs that made my hands alive with small tears, but I kept it around, hoping someday I would learn how to use it except I was lazy and never did.

My you, my you. Your insistent voice becomes the scrolling windows.

I lent it to a friend and she used it a lot more than I did—for letters and speeches. After a while I would come to her house and the you was a little more frayed than the last time. We pretended for a while that she would be giving it back but we both knew that it wasn't mine anymore.

Sometimes I actually got jealous and wished I had a you until I remembered how I had had one and neglected it. One day after a few glasses of wine, I told her I had no need for it and that she could keep it. After a few more glasses I told her that I did miss it a great deal and I took it back from her. After that night she stopped calling me and answering my emails.

I sentimentalized the you because to say you is warming. The you is irrelevant but still always within reach because I seldom do things without an audience. When I actually have it in my hands after leaving it under a pile of bills or laundry, the you looks to me with indifference.

The you insists that I engage lightly and instead I stomp around and wake the whole neighborhood with my boots to let everyone know what I think of the you's ideas.

It's not safe to bandy it around like we're all in on it. We're the opposite of in on it. We're inside and waving our little white flag.

Stockholm Syndrome

The city's banishment is the hand where I sleep like a foundling.
Yellow streetlights bristle against the grid, and I quiver like an obedient child.
I covet the stink of weed and funk in the hours before dawn—the worst time
since it's cool and barbaric. Then it's that morning of brackish soup
of which I would eat gallons. Once the city was a he, his arms around
our congress with enough alchemy to narcotize, eyes rolled back.
Once it was a she and we experimented with each other's tongues
because of anonymous and polymorphous. The radiant heaping dogshit
and its glaze on our skins, tastes of irony, of nickel. A newspaper drifts down
Mission Ave. and announces our new war, the folds alter the story. The broken glass,
a prism for the burdock in the cracks. Wrappers scuttle like living things,
skins shed of flesh. The half-sounds from my mouth are dirty with pathos,
with yellow neon. The alley, my polluted gullet. Launched
into this world poor and blind, I got hooked on turmoil and it's been costly.
Once on the edge of the ocean, I stepped on a bit of wood
with a nail in it, love-bite. The ocean stunned herself against the shore
because of our loneliness. Church bell sounded dusk to reify our seclusions.

Lunatics on My Avenue

At my window the present day bites into my ear with ideas I've liked before. The sun pushes in and out of the blue-green sphere that wavers on the edge of migraine, one, a mimicry of the other.

Lunatic: The circus geek, the Glad Bag man, the shrill and pocked face on the corner.

My street wears scars of real and unreal time but I'm afraid to leave my chair to see more closely. My lunatic crosses the street with all his futures. I see him every morning and take notes. Yesterday tucked in, today not. Today, seeming buoyant. Two days ago, dolorous.

The notes get tucked deep in my chair's cushion for the next day. My memory works with leniency, so I can see the outline of one lunatic through another though some have more jags.

This city gets settled by broken down fire dressed as someone else, and the lunatics follow with their dustpans.

My lunatic comes at night, the reason I don't sleep. He jeers when he walks past. It comes from far inside him, like his liver's hissing its name. I drop him down nothing because then he'll see me, too.

All of the lunatics' variations share equity of scale. At night they'll live in the warehouse, bunked up in tiny rows like the reflection of windows in apartments. My lunatic's the king. He gives the others maps and directions for making their way through the city, like where to lurch and what corners are good for cigarettes.

If my lunatic is a mirror, then he's opaque. Interference rises from the manholes in the form of smoke, and the interference colludes with the sun.

Let Down My Bucket

I kept hearing the small voice
describe what I was missing or
staying out of tonight: like

trees that howl and have
cooler things than arms.
I heard: Give in. Or easier:

Now.

(Like orange loves the sky
over a desert
I've broken open stones

looking for my part
or filled with all to be the planet
you want

I was disappear then come back,
disappear then come back)

Bay Bridge Abstraction

Not just a surface. Embedded horizontals,
the six-stroke face.
Five o'clock in the afternoon.
A dwindling black, high tide opened and entered:
glass blue. Vermilion hot, then white
turned over. The mirror is shut.

No mirrors. What we know hasn't got a body.
The curved sky is always a road
between us. Five thirty, the slack

chrome tripwire. Ochre blocks
recede the wall. The red slit down the left.
Difficult to say which is the sun.

The If of Omission

dayone:
At the edge of the attic: a solution. Do I wrap myself in tissue and tuck myself into the scrapbook that smells of vodka, of cigarettes, of industrial glue? If I could wriggle out of this geography, I'd memorize the future and bring it back to my progeny. Instead I'm harsh-voiced bridal party, a husk of that. My voice is so shrill. The lunatic calls and I can barely hold the phone.

dayten:
Fragrant kiss on my neck, Polaroid #3. Unlikely I'll find another photograph to tell the B side. The reparation provided to me is known as *eclectic beauty*. I catch my eye in the mirror, distract my very own loins. That helps the day pass, that taboo vaudeville.

dayonehundred:
I'm leaving my greasy print on all surfaces, even the superficial hi-bye friendship. And night falls, and the ocean swallows oil ships, and the deer die in our grilles— we're a series of mishaps, this vista and me. I swallow compassion from a blue round pill. It soothes my jaw and reminds me I'm not all edge.

daysevenhundred:
For years I've not taught anything shameful.

dayonethousand:
Little book of Syphilis. Epistolary book Written to the Latin's Ombudsman. The book of Irritating boils. The book of Soul-show-You-the-Door. The book of Gut-tersniping and Chivalry. book of yr. Deeds. Deeds to the Webb'd Hand. Tome on Inchoate Nations, Guide to Wax Seals And their Replicae, What and How of the Republic as told by a Rebel, A Mash note to Step Theory Disaster, how to Make A Quarantine, Encyclopedia of Creatures that Afflict, Dictionary of Ruin and Quilts, How to Gather 7 Horsewomyn, How to Finance yr. Pestilence. The Book of Books and in it, *chapter on Boats that Carry you to islands of Your Own Making.*

dayfivethousand:

If I could take myself up, if I could climb that vine, if I could give my passport to the Prez with my scent all over it, if I could sever the emollient impulse from my mane. If I had to travel without looking, if I dared mention names from the book of those days. If I could my hairs in your bed, and if you could your blood. If we had all been enough with the loaf split in half. If only I could have a large old bust of you, dilated with starpoints.

Civilizing Mission

As they came around me like a cloud with dictionaries, he said, *you're daughter to Aporia.* They bound me to this telling by my hair.

He whispered in my ear the definition of *hermetic* and urged I should change my sense of the hermetic.

She poured me into a cincture made from dollar bills. I barely moved. I was filthy and priceless. *A box of fruit,* they called me.

After some conversation they dipped me in water, head back like baptism. I babbled their language, and they gave me kisses as reward.

He tried to love me and I told him I was wed to Culture. When he felt my sagging breasts he was disillusioned. He said,

I thought you came well-built.

I got sprayed with smoke that killed me a little. They said it was *the Scent of Nature* and that it shouldn't hurt.

She said, *you'll get the proper stamps sometime*, but I didn't trust her except when eating from her hand. Her hand tasted like cigarettes and lemons and that made me wonder about her life.

One time they unfolded maps on emptied crates and pointed to the New World with their stub fingers. They said they wouldn't give up and that I shouldn't either. I thought this meant renewal and I reminded them I'd lain open longer than anyone else.

They left me alone at times and went into the corner to discuss. Whatever was said must have maddened because their faces came back complicated.

They said I was resistant. They said *it wouldn't come out.*

These are days and days passing, you understand. They were my undoing. A stretch, a fractal. It had started as play. We were going to switch at some point but didn't.

And wouldn't. I liked sleeping in the trundle next to them. They promised me a shining road and forks and just stuff. They gave me names to consider. They suggested *Kitten*.

Smaller, Quieter

I'm left with the desire to be as hard as a monster,
medieval mixed with inquisition and a dash
of troubadouress. You'll smell it in my black fur.
I'll be the apartment ghost: pass through walls,
through realism, but smaller, quieter,
the tumor in the center of your heart chakra.

Red Baroness

My sister sharpens her teeth
on the millstone around my neck.
This is our perfect union.
One of her feet is screwed to the floor
like the old joke. It allows her some
latitudes, and at the same time,
a core. We've been doing this for years,
both of us brands of failure,
but we do have some pinnacles.
Endurance is one.

THREE

Mistakes Were Made

About our last conversation, I misspoke. The story I heard was this: Once there was a prince, and he was a dunce. He left the windows opened during the storm and everyone in the castle drowned except for the rats.

I want to be austere, I do, but I wasn't built suchlike. That you forgive me is big of you. The story really was: Once the dunce-prince turned everyone into fish because he could. Some fish were old with heavy whiskers, and some were his friends, so they lived in the good coral. They weaned the coral into turrets with spikes.

I thought *to wean* meant something different. It's actually more fraught, and that's the polite word.

The story I remember: Once there was a queen who held a speck of filth in her hand because it entertained her, then the dunce-prince distracted her.

You may have heard the opposite. You may remember differently, as it was a contentious era. It might have two sides to it, one translucent and vulnerable, the other gritty as your tongue.

But enough with the rumors. The story really only was: *once there was a girl and she sucked life out of every marrowbone offered her.* And now I'm soft all around, and now you're a little bit old, a little bit loose in the chin, and you've lost it, haven't you? I still have the shrine of you and your foibles, still want to share a cell. Time is a different keeper for me. Toward you, between then and now, I walked in your shoes, double-time, because there was so much of you, dripping over the sides of me, the carnival we were.

Once there was a girl with long fingernails she used to kill her enemies. Years and years avenging old hurts. Then she got wrapped in a skein of silk and carried away by Eagle. I mean that to metaphorize the amateurs' terms for a golden mean.

My Fire and Fever Fussy

I thought, *I am drenched in regret.* I thought, *in the shower,*
I am wee. You thought, *the woman must be drunk and lonely.*

You thought, *purification takes her so long.* You thought,
surely she's in a baptism state. I thought, *my inherited disposition*

doesn't excuse all my gaffes but should. I thought, *five-six-seven-rinse.*
You thought, *if we are thrown down the cataract, will we be crushed?*

I thought, *everyone depends on me for certain pleasures.*
I'd like to be released into the city, but I'd be eaten whole.

You thought, *I stopped reading art for this. I climbed*
over barbed wire for this. I thought, *a penny saved*

is not enough for the twenty-first century, so let go of
agenda. You thought, *what part do I let loose? The media*

or the arts? Is this the zeitgeist trope?
I thought, *so I'll try better.* You thought, *then let's pretend*

the big thing never happened. I thought, *is it too late*
for church? You thought, *with hair gathering in the sink;*

she's growing old. I thought, *I am making myself over with scraps*
I steal from others. You thought, *open the windows*

and let out the roaches. I thought, *my art is waggish, sad. You*
can't have déjà vu by proxy, so we'll each earn our own revision.

Soft Power

I will say it base, you understand

Crossing a bridge and a narratologist tells me about harbors.
This is before I know you navigate your car through a landscape
of bridges. I've got an inkling of your smell. With that,
I decide to do everything right, knowing the magnitude
of that task. This was prior to your mouth.

This is what I mean

Egoista is how to say selfish. Ego: the self. –Ista like pharmacist
or philanthropist—one who traffics in the self. Last night,
I couldn't stop describing my flaws to you as serious
and possibly fatal, but you darned every incision.

Which is to say

I can tell you everything that ever happened
because it's already done. What about
what I am capable of? I'm afraid of the next day.

And we

We are a fascinating sum. We have been squared,
spliced, and negated. Our totals have been heaped
with words that don't equal.
(That's my hope talking, making us the same container.)

It must be obvious

I am vain and conceited. I steal. When I am scared, I lie.
I love the water curtain of opiates. I'd abandon you
for the trifling. I cry foolishly when I am in love. Broken things

in love. I don't know love. I love like a –philia.
I give love wrongly. I give it with spite and for greed.

Is that so bad?

I stuffed the gag of duplicity in your mouth,
and you bit into it. We were cruel probes.
We fixed the curtains
so dark would be ours for a time.
I saw you sleep,
so I saw you, my purgatory.

Forgive me, they were delicious

The windows are open. I speak through a fan
for the serration. I have a set of keys
to your house and to your car. I ride in your car
to the gas station with your money card.
I sit in your bedroom wrapped by your quilt.
I spill a circle of black ink, so not domestic,
and soak it with milk from your refrigerator,
and will be contrite and docile with you
and will leap at the sound of your
godwhistle at quitting time.

Ars Amatoria

(1) The disorderly display of kissing with tongue is now public. You tear through your Shakespeare for reference or pull on buttons with the edge of your fingernail or yell *you're so passive-aggressive* in the Indian restaurant. The origin has already launched itself outside of your orbit.

(2) She makes a promise she'll appear and then she doesn't. You wait outside the circus holding a balloon and she's savoring that moment because it's a war. You're made two slivers like brittle soap. The violence drives you to the sublime hell of your gaze. I recommend the city. You can dazzle and grift, disappear there. Leave the cell phone behind so you return to its pulse, pulse, pulse.

(3) You make it a lucid narrative and tell friends different bits and pieces. They help you put it back together like it's a puzzle. You amend the unjust parts and keep them as your own private scabs. Just don't end it with: *And then the light fell like shards of rain,* because no one will believe you.

(4) In an embrace, you'll find the sweet spot at the knuckle of the neck, under the scapula, in the fold of the armpit, and mark it with a flag of spit and your nail sickle. Not just sinful, but coarse and profane animal behavior.

(5) You'll say *we won't fight around other people* and you fight around other people. Shameful, what you toss in the other's face.

(6) You refer to everything through cinema, say, *this is so* Before Sunrise or *I had a* Last Tango in Paris *yesterday*. You'll blush. You'll twist away. Oh, the trash you'll read in magazines as scripture! The odds and ends of mania.

(7) Is it not what your mother once told you about the cow and the milk? Mad love? Yes and no. She lives on the surface having risen years earlier from its depths. Your mother considers your situation from a terribly myopic vantage point, trainspotter.

(8) He leans his head and makes a moment so rare it's sacred. Or a mouth opens just so that you tangle in a hotel with strangers. The lighting of a lighter becomes hypnosis. Hair is disguise. The plumb line of an off-kilter face makes a bridge into you drowning in blue iris.

(9) You get violet thinking about it, drop by drop, absolutely violet. How will you fuck it up? How will you throw it in the rubbish bin of life? There's no atonement. If you play the piano, that might work. If you make more money, that might work. Even at the beginning lives the end. It starts to die when it starts. The thrill of this is you do it anyway because dying isn't so bad.

(10) Waiters are the most dangerous of men.

(11) The only depth: your undertow, your anesthetic. You scratch at your neck like Ophelia and her total drown high.

(12) To trounce, to pounce. To conquer, to vanquish. To domesticate, to fever. To defeat, to occupy. You're transitive with a capital S. Bring a handkerchief and a steady hand. Bring taming stories, lots of self-pity. Bring fancy scarves to use as ties. Bring pillows and Viagra. Bring recipes featuring scallops and turmeric. Bring recipes featuring mint and lamb. Bring muzzles and tiny boxes of shells collected on weekend getaways.

(13) Mumbles on the phone. Sexting. Codependency and its tedium.

(14) You leave parts of yourself all over the nation. Bits in Northern California, in the far south of New Mexico, Iowa, Paris, Cuernavaca: bits to leave the grackles because they live off of the cast-off flecks of your core.

(15) You start as strangers with each one and they become a compartment in you with her habits and her sweaters, with all his stray bits: a Cornell box in you, the wreckage, each of the hims, the hers, the them.

The Terms

When the telephone rings, I let it ring; it's a term of my exile. I can allow ten feet of rope out the window and only four birds may visit the telephone wires outside. *Figure it out*, they tell me.

I can't look forward or to the future or to the door of eggs and wives, and only three hold jailer's keys. My hands, coy companions, look terrifying now, like claws or cloying snakes.

If the window is open and a parade passes, then I must close the window. Some terms involve windows, although I only have one.

Terms about how much I can say about the president. About how many cigarettes I can smoke. The length of my veil. Can I play Aaron Copland at five? One that insists I read recovery narratives: tracts in yellow ink.

My exile has terms that aren't proscribed. Pushed out of shape and stretched, a price I fret over like the mishap of my hands over my face, the metropolitan succubus.

I can tell my past with abstract brushstrokes only. Black or white. I can't even give a detail, tell you I was too young to see what I did, or about the length of my reveries. I am to memorize old maxims, then apply them as curative to my impertinent torso.

Don't Get Out Much Anymore

Fear of heteroglossia.
Fear of mail fraud.
Fear of carpeted stairs.
Fear of being perceived as phony-allergic.
Fear of noun plague.
Fear of magazines about walking.
Fear of mispronounced tenderness.
Fear of pens with chewed blue caps.
Fear of the memory lacquer.
Fear of stale cookie cups.
Fear of celebrity cellulite.
Fear of exile.
Fear of the vengeful God.
Fear of the slag curves of compact fluorescents.
Fear of lost Monopoly pieces.
Fear of the unsalvageable CD.
Fear of the memory that loops.
Fear of the empty telephone.
Fear of the metal coil of your notebook.
Fear of public bleeding.
Fear of your painter friend.
Fear of Hummers.
Fear of nickels.
Fear of white rooms.
Fear of the fear that the current takes you.
Fear of the songbook.
Fear of pencil shavings from the workday.

Rival

I came to know my rival's name when it got posted on the billboard across the street. I saw them come and take down the old one pasting up my rival's golden hair first.

Each tendril was as thick as my wrist, four or five shades of yellow in the picture. I couldn't see her left ear with all that hair, but an earring, a ruby. We live in a windy city, so they could barely tame her face. One man held one corner and pinned it back. The other man pulled his end taut while this went down. He patted her rouged cheek.

It was just the face and not the body. Her mouth was big as a lifeboat, like she could save us. Her giant eyes followed me like the Mona Lisa. I stared long to see if I could know her, so much I came to know her story. Then we were connected.

It was spiritual. We began to look alike, her face as mine. I adopted her remote and pristine mannerism.

Eventually I wrote her to tell her about the goings-on outside my window. Since I had her audience I also told her about my grief collection. I felt like I could tell her anything and I did. I began at the beginning, spelling out for her the twists and turns of my exile.

I told her that I called myself Rapunzel after our long hair. I took pictures of her from every angle so she could see what I see.

The letter took me months and meanwhile her face disintegrated with the weather, bits and pieces of my Dorian Gray.

My Open Sesame

The lyric tires me because
it's so familiar and open-mouthed.
But stars—my default,
a subversion of subversion.
I got trained for this affect
in the best schools by gray
masters where awards were easy
to imagine as arrival.

Crepuscular wind, take me back
to a wet and slithering modern
or at least acknowledge the rift
because I'm unrepentant.
To throw fire into the kerfuffle
is my wet dream. To anticipate
the end times, my nerdgasm.
(See? Do you recognize the vulnerability?
I hope someone writes about it on his blog.)

Redaction

We make dogma out of letter writing: the apocryphal story
of Lincoln who wrote angry letters he never sent. We wait for letters
for days and days. Someone tells me, *I'll write you a letter*
and I feel he's saying, *you're so different from anyone else.*
Distance's buzz gets louder and louder. It gets to be a blackest hole.
I want the letter about the time we cross the avenue, and you reach
for my hand without looking—I am afraid I'm not what you want.
We float down the street as if in the curve of a pod
and the starry black is like the inside of a secret. We're drunk.
The streetlight exposes us, which becomes the deepest
horror. Yes. End the letter like that, so it becomes authorless.
Then the letter might give off secrets: acid imbalances that detonate.

Under a Wan Sun

Blue gets plucked from the dresser for today's
costume. I'm feeling demure, so I want
the faux-priss of the opera-princess-drag queen.

The days have woven gray into my hair,
have over-ripened. I'm saving my pennies
to inject poison into the lines that extend from
my nose to my mouth, lines I hadn't noticed
until it was too late. My lithe Mallarméan hand
stirs up the violence of time, reminds me that all
things go in particles out of the windows. I am
disappearing bit by bit, and what's left, *pink*.

Red gets drawn from the drawer for today's
costume. If I stand at the window I stop
traffic with my semaphoric vamping.
All of Van Ness backed into a corner
for my layered, complex gender play.

Lavender for giggles. Gray for lightbulbs.
This is my bargain with mortality because
John Belushi is dead. Angela Carter
is dead. Samuel Beckett is dead. Mama Cass,
dead. Laura Riding Jackson is dead.
Marvin Gaye. Gabriela Mistral. Soupy Sales.

Turquoise gets drawn from the drawer for bourgie
pretense. Imagine the ruin of my testament if I get asked.
I've got an appointment with someone who knows.
Benjamin, dead. Grandmother, dead.
Maybe I'll add a dash of purple to my costume,
my itinerary. I'll add the puce of my Thanatos
hoping to drain the neighbor's mortality.

Malaprops

This effusion of words would take more than just measuring. I think volumes, but I'm shown *walls covered with it*. Aloud is when my words make a mark inscribed in round pastel globes like musical notation, then bits of rage in India ink. Words in Sharpie, in fountain pen filigree I read as apocryphal because they describe my dulcet evasions, my good and pretty story. I get a chance to review.

I count the *memes* because I want to know when that conceit started. *That was sweet, all mine*, then *cut it for me,* then, *I don't trust the postman. Flea bite.* I count these too. I make redactions and elisions to undo the past just enough. Do you know what I mean by that? Not just the grandfather paradox. I want to keep it bruising and felt, a red aura around my lies and the pale glyphs of obedience. Yet I also want to be loved by all. I want forgiveness idiom.

I shift names and add emphases. I revise decisions; make no into yes in the hopes I might change the brutal and the torrid. Do I muddle the story? Do I make the plot a Rorschach? This wall's pulsing with alteration because I'm always saying in flashes thrown up behind my back. I complicate, I derange. I make such dramatic diction shifts that the walls' gypsum just fumes and smokes with red tag violations.

Sometimes There's a Virgin

Sometimes there's a virgin in the room.
You make way for her light; she is
fountainhead. When the virgin is in the room,
she's robed by dim wattage. Virgin, remind me.
When the virgin is in the room, our skirts
feel tarty, when there's a virgin in the room.
The virgin has clean hair and there's nothing
under her fingernails. She drinks water from the same
cup all night long. She writes her name on the cup.
The virgin writes lyric poetry about roads and wars
and the crown of trees but has a degree
in something outside the arts because artists
aren't virgins. Everyone talks to her and she doesn't even
have mascara on; her eyelashes are naturally thick.
I brush past her to feel virginity. There's a big
difference between virgin and non-virgin, aura-wise.
Someone drives her home before eleven o'clock.
The virgin has a long driveway
at her house; a parent waits for her.
The virgin leaves her vibe behind, so we wait
for it to dissipate. Then we get nasty and high since
the virgin made us feel bad because we gave it up
in high school. That's just her course. It's not our fault.

These Halting Plaints

I am blameless but not blameless.
I am pristine but not pristine.
I am hugged but not hugged,
all of us not hugged. All of us teem
with shame but most of all me.
I am plutonium but not that matter.
I am with a curse on my head but not vexed
by it. I am made a diffuse powder by grief
but not spread over the city.
Splinter but not aching.
Albatross but not dead. Am love
but did not. I am policy but not nervy.
Peninsula but not district.
These halting plaints remain basis
for the teeming discord I am,
a patient with a gram of mutiny.

Don't I Disappear

Come asleep,
come purple deep.
Come firmament,
I sweeten the breach.

I'll hold you in my lap.
You'll be my gull, one bird
for the whole year.

Down one length, a pull.
Down another, the one art.
This path's an alphabet.
Each stone, a sound
from your gorge.

Your mouth is a fact,
also a settlement,
fugitive sensation I resist.
A crime, finally, the abyss
and your same smeared mouth.

My Hegemony

Another godsend. I make it good.

A critique of romantic love with lots of parking, no meters.

Enough with unmanned ships. We're in it to win it.

Jingo, jingo, jingo.

The dog-faced girl will lead us to the water and convert seed to coin.

We won't need the seed, though. We've got test tubes.

Does anyone remember the theme of the last overthrow? It had something
to do with Greek tragedy.

The Swedish Commune Utopia ChildCare Program for Leftists.

You'll want to take that call.

She'll unfacet her diamond when we need it for murder.

When she has the bluster and the grit, we build legislation around it, then free
agent in under ten minutes!

Or we make all lucre worthless except as material for building edifice.

The Camera Analysis of Streets for the Daughters Project.

Because I said so.

Sometimes smoking on the porch and in airplanes for the seventies feel.

That memory becomes tape dispenser. That your transference does, too.

We'll live in poems that drown in self-awareness, and then live in poems
that drown in the treacle of subjectivity.

Dissent will kill me, but I tie a rope around my waist to jump into the sharky waters.

Between the oracle and the MC, I'll choose the one of dubious origin.

A Venn diagram of desire for boys AND girls. In the middle, sushi and digital sounds.

The Sincerity gauntlet at the airport.

Is it okay to say Bible in here?

Anodyne

Today I slip away for an excursion into the landscape on the wall.
It's called,
Nothing good ever happens here.

A deer stares from the woods after being chased from the garden,
eyes tiny and piercing.
The only window is a wavering box
of gray paint in all the red and below all of it, a signature in a 1930s cursive—
trembly and sincere.

I write at a desk in the corner of the barn where I can practically not exist.

My fingerbones creak because of *the thing* that eludes.
I thought I would be open, but language has shut me out. The painting's silence
is defeating.

What I'm working on (rough draft): A potion to lick off. Autumn was a place.
Crumb & crumb.   I made a swear word.
When winter comes, you see the end of days.

My favorite part is the space between the *crumb* and the *I*. I'd like what I write
to reach into the center of the pastoral and throttle it, but the painting resists.
To really pummel the barn, to make a pulp of 19th-century agriculture,
but the painting wants to be just itself
and won't let me elevate us. I would like us to slip into the unknowing,
the abyss, such a benign force to bear against. On some days
I can't leave it even though the hum of censure overpowers like skunk.
When I sit outside it, no bees seem alive.

To My Book

You'll get a slice: the filigree of my fingerprint
on a glass slide, vial of my murkiest bile, petri dish of phlegm,
most acidic saliva, two jars; one of urine, the other my
dense evacuation—narratives of my gluttony, a fingernail
and its dirty furrows. A strand of hair and its rings.

Two blood ampoules: one drawn from a cut to the lip,
the other menstrual and tentacled. From my spine,
a tiny bottle of cloudy vigor—the thoroughfare's dredge.
Pictures of my bones and their gaps, each as lack
or degeneration, obscure or ample. My blood's index,

O positive, its counts and ingredients. Pictures of my viscera,
each organ's pulsing humor,
my brain's impulses mapped like the Metro:
red for frenzy, blue for cold wet study. From beneath my umbilicus,
clammy seeds for the test tube, for the long sequence of sequences.

You'll have eternal decay stitched into
your binding, my invocation, manifesto,
my weighty xxoo.

Notes

The title "These Halting Plaints," the line "My art is waggish, sad," and the line "For years I've not taught anything shameful" are from Ovid's *Poems of Exile*.

The title "The Science of Parting" is from Osip Mandlestam's *Tristia*.

The title "My Fire and Fever Fussy" is from Gerard Manley Hopkins's poem "In Honour of St. Alphonsus Rodriguez."

The title "My Open Sesame" is from Wayne Koestenbaum's essay "My 80s."

Acknowledgments

Many thanks to the editors who published these poems in the following publications: *26, A Public Space, Barn Owl Review, Bone Bouquet, Boston Review, Brooklyn Rail, Coconut Poetry, Colorado Review, Denver Quarterly, Eleven Eleven, Equalizer, Fairy Tale Review, H_NGM_N, jubilat, New American Writing, Oranges & Sardines, Palabra, Pilgrimage, Poetry, Sleepingfish, Tusculum Review,* and *Whiskey Train.*

This book is set in Bulmer and Gill Sans Condensed by the Center for Literary Publishing at Colorado State University. Copyediting by Joanna Doxey. Proofreading by Haley Larson. Book design and typsetting by Christopher Klingbeil. Cover design by Kir Jordan. Printing by BookMobile.